CLAVIER-BÜCHLEIN VOR WILHELM FRIEDEMANN BACH

Da Capo Press Music Reprint Series

MUSIC EDITOR
BEA FRIEDLAND
Ph.D., City University of New York

JOHANN SEBASTIAN BACH

CLAVIER-BÜCHLEIN VOR WILHELM FRIEDEMANN BACH

EDITED IN FACSIMILE WITH A PREFACE BY RALPH KIRKPATRICK

DA CAPO PRESS · NEW YORK · 1979

Library of Congress Cataloging in Publication Data

Bach, Johann Sebastian, 1685-1750.
  Clavier-Büchlein vor Wilhelm Friedemann Bach.

  (Da Capo Press music reprint series)
  Reprint of the 1959 ed. published by Yale University
Press, New Haven.
  Reproduced from the holograph, principally in the
hand of J. S. Bach, in the Library of the School of
Music, Yale University; on t.p. of holography:
"angefangen in Cöthen den 22. Januar Aö. 1720."
  Bibliography: p.
  1. Harpsichord music. 2. Bach, Wilhelm Friedemann,
1710-1784. II. Kirkpatrick, Ralph. III. Title.
[ML96.5.B186 1979 case] [M22] 786.4′05′4 79-11313
ISBN 0-306-79558-2

This Da Capo Press edition of *Clavier-Büchlein Vor
Wilhelm Friedemann Bach* is an unabridged republication
of the edition published in New Haven in 1959.

Published by Da Capo Press, Inc.
A Subsidiary of Plenum Publishing Corporation
227 West 17th Street, New York, N.Y. 10011

CLAVIER-BÜCHLEIN VOR WILHELM FRIEDEMANN BACH

JOHANN SEBASTIAN BACH

CLAVIER-BÜCHLEIN VOR WILHELM FRIEDEMANN BACH

EDITED IN FACSIMILE WITH A PREFACE BY RALPH KIRKPATRICK

NEW HAVEN: YALE UNIVERSITY PRESS 1959

Editorial matter © 1959 by Yale University Press, Inc.
Printed in the United States of America by
The Meriden Gravure Company, Meriden, Conn.,
by photo offset lithography, with 300-line screen.
Library of Congress catalog card number: 58–11407

CONTENTS

DESCRIPTIVE NOTE   149

BIBLIOGRAPHICAL NOTE   151

BIBLIOGRAPHY   153

PREFACE

The Clavier-Büchlein vor Wilhelm Friedemann Bach is a modest little volume bound in board covered with thin parchment. On the paper lining pasted to the inside of the front cover J. S. Bach has written the title: "Clavier-Büchlein / vor / Wilhelm Friedemann Bach. / angefangen in / Cöthen den / 22. Januar / Aõ. 1720." ("Little Clavier-Book for Wilhelm Friedemann Bach, begun in Cöthen on January 22 in the year 1720.") Friedemann Bach's name appears again, scrawled on the paper lining of the back cover. He was Bach's eldest son, and a little over nine years old at the time the Clavier-Büchlein was begun. The book contains sixty-two pieces written into it almost entirely by Bach and his son. Among them are seven of Bach's Little Preludes, eleven of the preludes of the Well-Tempered Clavier, the two-part Inventions and the three-part Sinfonias, as well as a few works by other composers. The beginning of the book is in J. S. Bach's handwriting, the middle in Friedemann's, with considerable alteration and collaboration by his father, and the end of the book is entirely in J. S. Bach's hand. There is evidence both at the beginning and at the end of the book that it was already bound up at the time of writing. Its dimensions are the same as those of the present facsimile.

On the front flyleaf appears the inscription: "This book is a rarity, for it is written by the great S. Bach and comes from the estate of the late so-called Clavier-Bach of the Pädag. in Halle, along with much Bach and other music and pictures from the Bach family, bought by me in the year 1814. J. Koetschau."

Koetschau was *Musikdirektor* in Schulpforte, and the "so-called Clavier-Bach" was a Johann Christian Bach, a distant cousin of Friedemann Bach, who had obtained the Clavier-Büchlein from Friedemann. At the auctioning of Koetschau's library in 1845 the Clavier-Büchlein passed into the possession of the Krug family in Naumburg, later Freiburg im Breisgau. In 1932 it was bought from Siegfried Krug of Diessen (Ammersee) by the Library of the Yale School of Music. The present facsimile publication has been greatly aided by the librarian, Brooks Shepard, Jr., and his staff, and by his predecessor Miss Eva J. O'Meara, under whose auspices the Clavier-Büchlein was acquired.

The beginning of the Clavier-Büchlein has an avowedly pedagogic character. The first page presents a codification of the various clefs and gives the nomenclature of the notes in various octaves. Immediately following, there appears Bach's famous table of ornaments, an "Explanation of various signs, showing how to play certain ornaments correctly." This table bears witness to the French origins of most of Bach's ornamentation in that its examples are very similar to those in the table preceding the Pièces de Clavecin of J. H. d'Anglebert in the Paris edition of 1689.

The pedagogical tone is maintained for a time through subsequent sections of the Clavier-Büchlein, but it soon becomes clear that we have here not an *a priori* organized method of instruction but rather a collection of pieces that reflect only fragmentarily and to a certain extent haphazardly the intense musical life of the Bach household. It is plain that Friedemann Bach received much more musical instruction than is noted in the Clavier-Büchlein and that his musical experience before and during its compilation was much richer than is there directly indicated. However the Clavier-Büchlein records with a beguiling intimacy certain moments in Bach's concern with his son's musical education, certain evidences of his guiding and collaborating hand; and later, when it becomes less an instruction book than a repository for certain pieces with which Bach or his son was preoccupied, the first draft of the three-part Sinfonias admits us to creative moments of a blistering intensity.

In Bach's sense, all the pieces in the Clavier-Büchlein have a pedagogical purpose, although they are not at all organized as in the piano methods of a later day. In the first place, Bach and his contemporaries never separated keyboard playing from creative musical thinking. The elements of fingering and of keyboard technique were from the beginning associated with continuo playing and with free improvisation, thus opening the way into formal musical composition. Gerber (I, 491–492) records of his father that Bach first taught him Inventions, then suites, and finally the Well-Tempered Clavier. Forkel (pp. 58–59) expands on similar reports and mentions Bach's writing down small pieces for his pupils. This implies no mere technical progression of finger exercises such as far too much Bach music later became, but rather a progression of musical perception and of capacity for musical thought. It is in this spirit that Bach himself calls the study of his Inventions and Sinfonias a "foretaste of composition."

Out of my own experience merely as a keyboard teacher I can testify that with a new pupil, no matter how dazzling a digital competence he may bring, I usually need to spend four to six months on the twelve Little Preludes and a handful of Inventions and Sinfonias before I am satisfied that his ear and musical feeling have searched them to the best of his capacity, and that he has found out how to express on a keyboard the essentials of what he has learned to hear and feel. Once he is past the Inventions, supplemented by the relaxing reassurance of freer preludes and dance pieces, occasionally also by refreshing excursions into other styles; once a few three- and four-voice fugues have been thoroughly heard, sung in every note and every voice, and impeccably fingered—things move very fast indeed toward a fusion of keyboard competence and musical understanding.

Headed by the pious inscription I.N.I. [*In Nomine Jesu*], the music of the Clavier-Büchlein begins with a little piece called Applicatio. True to its name it is almost completely supplied with indications for fingering. Bach still uses here the old style of fingering that had been universally in vogue since the sixteenth century and that lasted, side by side with more modern innovations, well into the end of the eighteenth. As the Applicatio demonstrates, scale passages in this style are fingered with a longer finger crossing over a shorter, except that for ascending passages the left hand alternates thumb and index finger. Only two other examples of Bach's fingering are known, a Little Prelude in G minor that occurs later in the Clavier-Büchlein, and an early version of the first prelude and fugue of Book II of the Well-Tempered Clavier that is published in Volume XXXVI of the Bachgesellschaft edition.

Immediately after the Applicatio comes a Praeambulum in C major which is recognizable as the first of what we now know in a late eighteenth-century compilation as the Twelve Little Preludes. Practical application of Bach's prefatory table of ornaments is to be found in this piece and in the decorated setting of *Wer nur den lieben Gott lässt walten* which follows. Next comes a Little Prelude in D minor, then an incomplete decorated version of *Jesu meine Freude*. All these pieces are in J. S. Bach's hand.

The two chorales are the only pieces in the Clavier-Büchlein that remind us of the organ, but there is plenty of precedent for their being played on any sort of household keyboard instrument. Except for the designation of the harpsichord that later heads a piece by J. C. Richter, the Clavier-Büchlein makes no reference to any specific keyboard instrument and there is not sufficient evidence to indicate an exclusive choice either of harpsichord or clavichord.

A change in the character of the writing confronts us in the next two Allemandes, the second of which lacks its conclusion. They have all the appearance of being composition studies of Friedemann's made under the supervision of his father. J. S. Bach's hand has been detected in the titles and incipits and in interventions in Friedemann's writing of the text. (It should be stated here that all our attributions of handwriting are based on the researches and kindness of Wolfgang Plath, the editor of the Clavier-Büchlein for its forthcoming publication in the Neue Bach Ausgabe.)

Friedemann's hand continues alone in the next of the Little Preludes and his father takes over with two more, the first of which is almost fully fingered. Three Menuets then appear, the first in Friedemann's hand, the last in that of his father, and the middle one in what has been seen as a collaboration of both. The first of the Menuets was also copied into the Clavier-Büchlein begun in 1722 for Friedemann's stepmother Anna Magdalena Bach. (Friedemann's mother had died in July 1720, not long after the beginning of the Clavier-Büchlein, and his father had married again in December 1721.)

The next section of the book brings eleven of the preludes of Book I of the Well-Tempered Clavier, written out by Friedemann with occasional contributions by his father both to titles and texts. The first seven are numbered in ascending diatonic order and include four preludes in less fully developed versions than those we now know. It is interesting to note the tentativeness of the C major prelude, and the absence of the pedal points that later swell out the C minor and D minor preludes; but the Clavier-Büchlein version of the E minor prelude is perhaps the most revealing of Bach's habit of elaborating a simple harmonic structure. Not only is the animated coda of the later version absent, but the florid cantilena of the opening has not yet emerged. Instead, a mere chordal continuo realization is still completely dominated by the ostinato moving bass. A curious feature at the end of this version is the annotation "volti Prae:" that seems to lead directly to the ensuing

E major prelude. Presumably the copying out of these preludes in the Clavier-Büchlein considerably antedates Bach's compilation of the first book of the Well-Tempered Clavier in 1722.

Of the eleven preludes copied into the Clavier-Büchlein four come to a halt at the end of a page with no sign of any attempted conclusion, even when the adding of extra staves at the bottom of the page would have permitted it. The book shows signs of use throughout, especially on the lower page-turning corners. Was Friedemann content to recollect the end of a piece approximately, or did his father allow him to leave these pieces incomplete as an encouragement to improvising fitting conclusions? One can hardly believe, however, that the incompletenesses of the Clavier-Büchlein were deliberate.

The middle of the book is occupied by a miscellaneous series of complete and incomplete pieces, and by a number of pages left empty. Friedemann's transcript of a *Pièce pour le Clavecin, composée par J. C. Richter* (probably the Richter who in 1726 was court organist in Dresden) breaks off both in its Allemande and in its Courante. Then, following an empty page, there appear three pieces in Friedemann's hand, a prelude in C so closely related as almost to constitute a variant of the first in the book, a prelude in D that we know from the Twelve Little Preludes, and another prelude in E minor that is broken off immediately before an empty page. The next three pieces are all separated by empty pages. The first, in Friedemann's hand, is a curious little prelude of obvious French origin, followed on an otherwise empty page by an initial bracket with clef signs. Then comes a sketch in an unknown hand of a bare bass part that is certainly not by Bach. The last piece of this section is a three-voice fugue in J. S. Bach's hand. (Wolfgang Plath suggests that the pieces of the foregoing section were copied in after the end of the book had already been filled up. His forthcoming text revision promises a detailed analysis of the handwriting in the Clavier-Büchlein.)

The book now takes on a more definite direction. A series of fifteen pieces, each called Praeambulum, brings us the earliest known version of the two-part Inventions. Their order, unlike that familiar to us in the latest version, follows here the ascending diatonic scale: C major, D minor, E minor, F major, G major, A minor, B minor, with the remaining pieces arranged in descending order of tonality from B flat major down to C minor. In this series, and henceforth until the breaking off of the last piece in the book, all movements are complete. J. S. Bach's hand has been detected in the first two Praeambulae, but the next five are in Friedemann's. It is after the completion of the ascending series of seven Praeambulae that J. S. Bach definitely takes over for the remaining eight of the descending series and that the writing shows increasing signs of proximity to the creative process.

After the fifteen Praeambulae comes an interlude in Friedemann's hand consisting of three unattributed dance movements now certainly ascribable to Telemann, and a Partita by G. H. Stoelzel (1690–1749). For the Menuet of Stoelzel's Partita J. S. Bach has written in a Trio which we know as one of the Little Preludes.

The end of the book is devoted to the three-part Sinfonias, very probably in their first writing-down. Here each piece is called a Fantasia. They follow the same order of keys as the fifteen two-part Praeambulae, but the series is incomplete, for the music of the book now comes to an end in the middle of the D major Fantasia, lacking altogether the C minor, which would have been the last. Bach's handwriting is particularly revealing here. From one piece to another it undergoes many of the same changes in character as do the pieces themselves. A study of these pages should induce many a performer to reconsider his interpretations. Moreover the order of the Fantasias here, and the succession of characters they represent, might conceivably correspond to the succession of moods according to which they were actually composed.

In some of the pieces one senses the urgency of the direct physical utterance, even the way in which breath is taken; one recognizes the origin of the music in a specific physical organism. Anyone who has ever heard a great composer sing his own fugue subject will know what I mean. And what shall I say of the handwriting in the F minor Fantasia? Is this not the kind of thing that is written with more than ink? Was ever double counterpoint set on paper with greater intensity? Then turn the page to the smiling relaxation of the E major Fantasia!

Variants turn up in this text that explain many inflections in the later version, and the largely undecorated version of the E flat Fantasia hints at the freedom with which it was expected to be treated. The A minor Fantasia reveals a system of barring that couples two 3/8 measures into a 6/8 throughout, and a glance at the handwriting of the B minor Fantasia might make a performer ask himself if he has not been playing it too fast!

Bach's writing of the Fantasias into the Clavier-Büchlein must have somewhat antedated his preparing of the complete final copy of the Inventions and Sinfonias early in 1723, just before he gave up his position in Cöthen and moved to Leipzig. This final copy was inherited by Carl Philipp Emanuel Bach. It is noteworthy that the son of Bach who most strikingly carried on the great pedagogical tradition into the next generation was not Friedemann, but Carl Philipp Emanuel Bach in his own independent way, with his admirable and influential *Versuch über die wahre Art das Clavier zu spielen.*

One of the charms of the Clavier-Büchlein is the fact that it was never intended for the outside world. Another is the opportunity it affords for fantasies reconstructing the musical activities of the Bach family, though such reconstructions are often all too easily demolished by a casually aimed fact. The manifold ambiguities and inconsistencies of the Clavier-Büchlein are very much like those of certain well-worn household objects associated with a great deal of living. Like the notebooks for Anna Magdalena Bach, this little book has an informality and a warmth that brings us in some ways far closer to Bach than the balanced monumentality of presentation autographs like that of the Brandenburg Concertos or the official fair copies of certain clavier and organ works. Even the most familiar pieces seem here to take on the added freshness and fluidity that come with proximity to the creative process. Moreover one is blessedly unaware of having an aura of greatness to penetrate. The imposing frown of official portraits has broken, as it were, into a smile of welcome into the workshop and into the family circle.

RALPH KIRKPATRICK

Yale University
1958

THE CLAVIER-BÜCHLEIN IN FACSIMILE

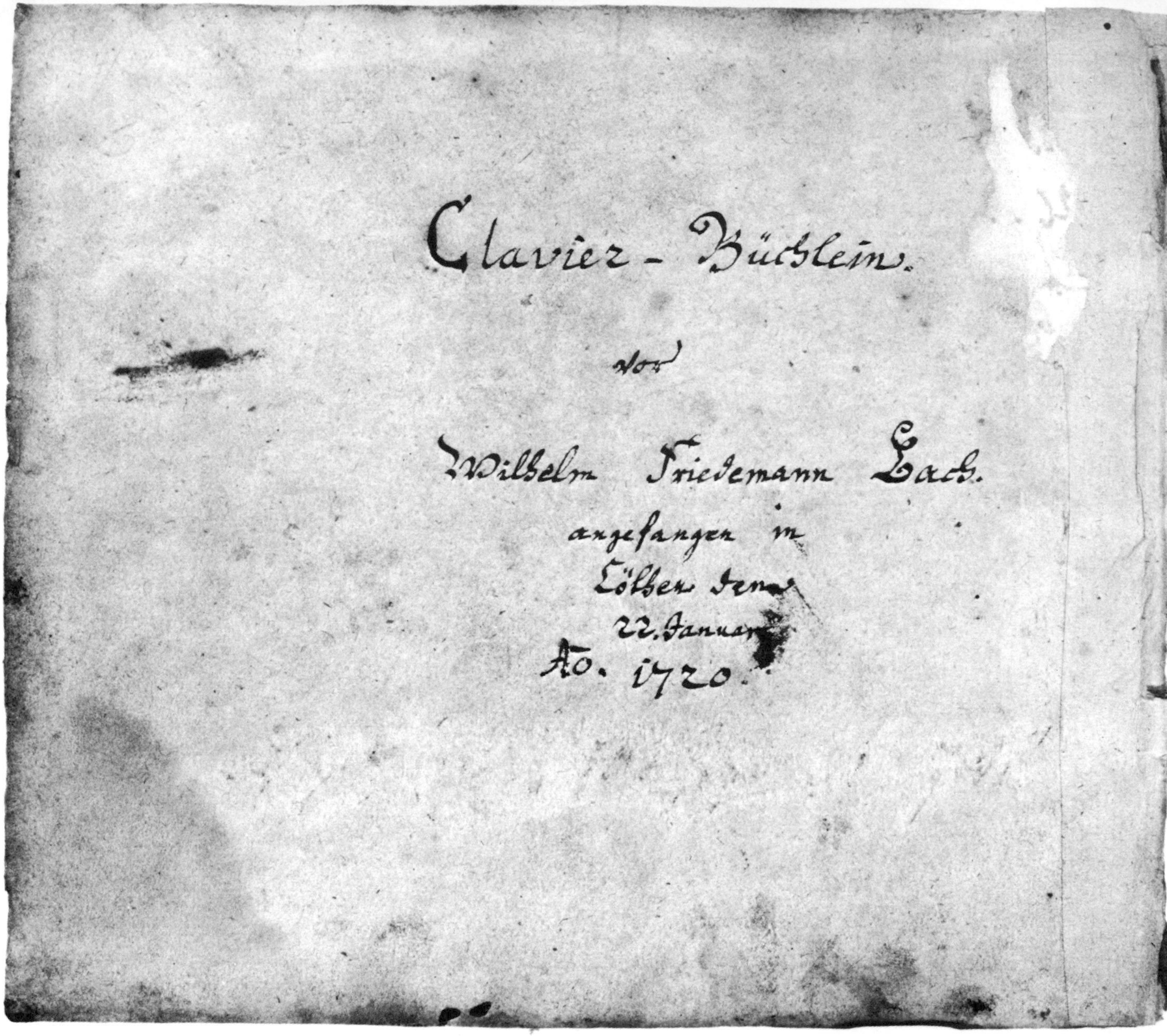

Clavier-Büchlein.

vor

Wilhelm Friedemann Bach.

angefangen in
Cöthen den
22. Januar
Ao. 1720

Dieses Buch ist mein Eigenthum, das aber von
dem sel. H. Bach geschrieb, u. aus dem Nachlaß
des verstorbenen sogenannten Clavier-Bachs auf dem
Pädag. zu Halle, nebst einigen Bachschen musikalis. u.
Bildern aus der B. familie von mir im
Jahre 1817 gekauft worden.

J. Westphal.

6

Explication unterschiedlicher Zeichen, so gewiße manieren artig zu spielen, andeüten.

Applicatio -

Præambulum.

14

+Allemande.

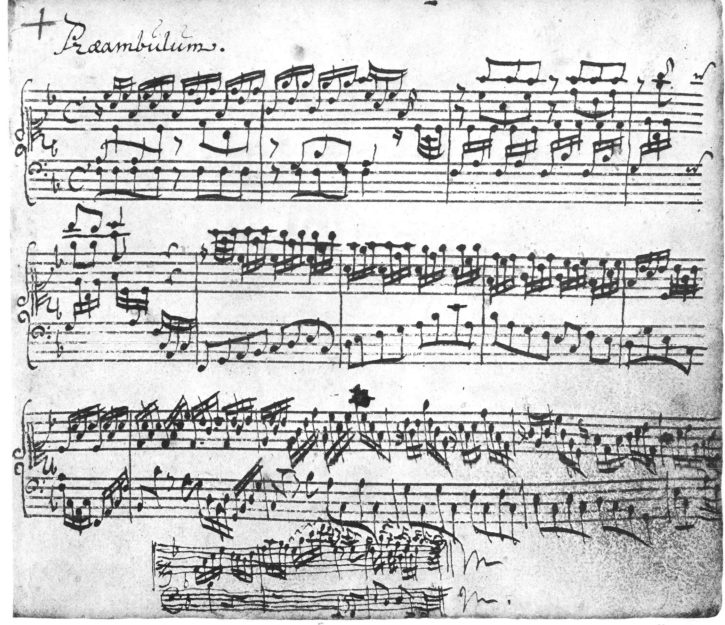

Præludium

29

Praeludium 2.

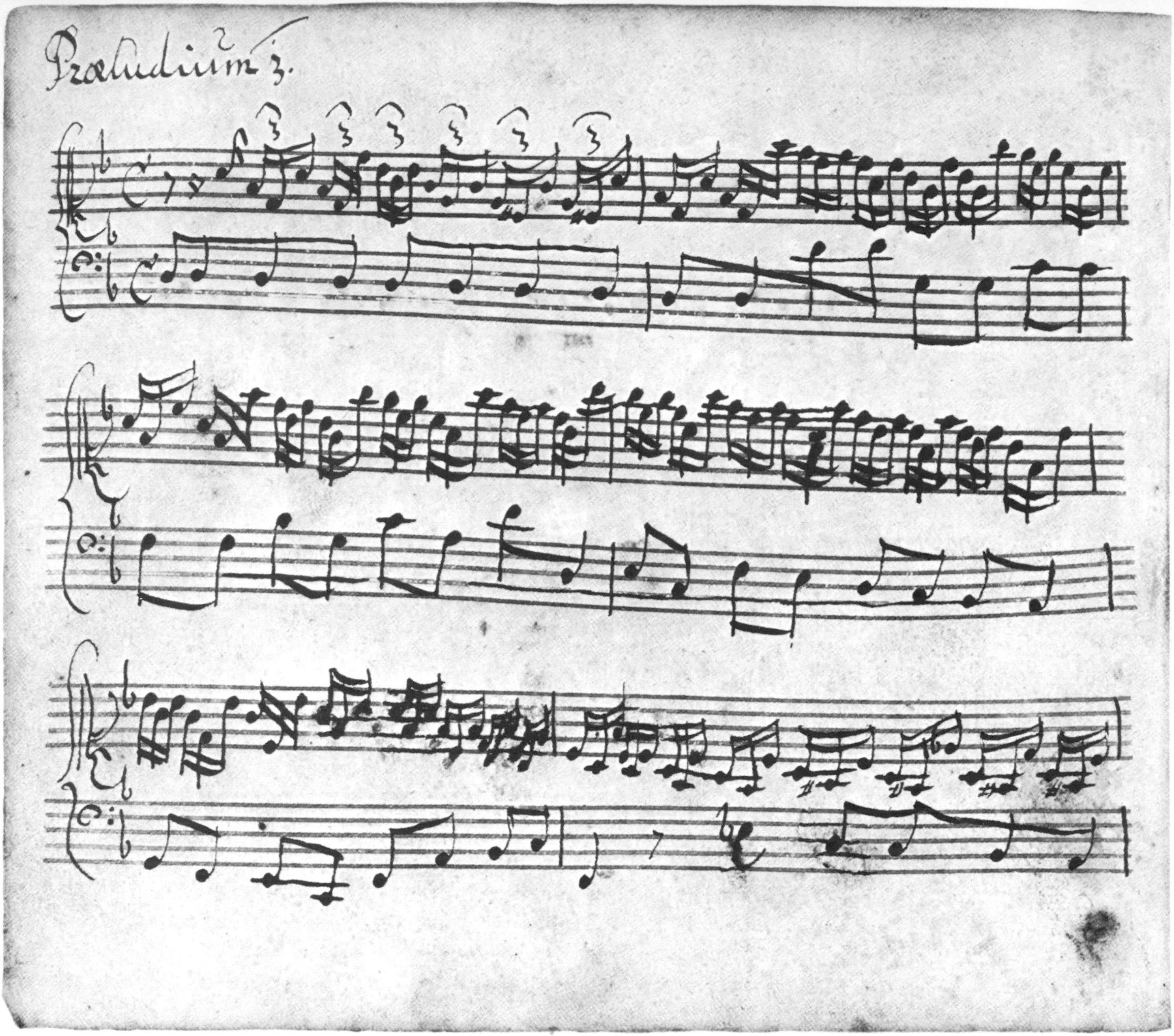
Præludium 3.

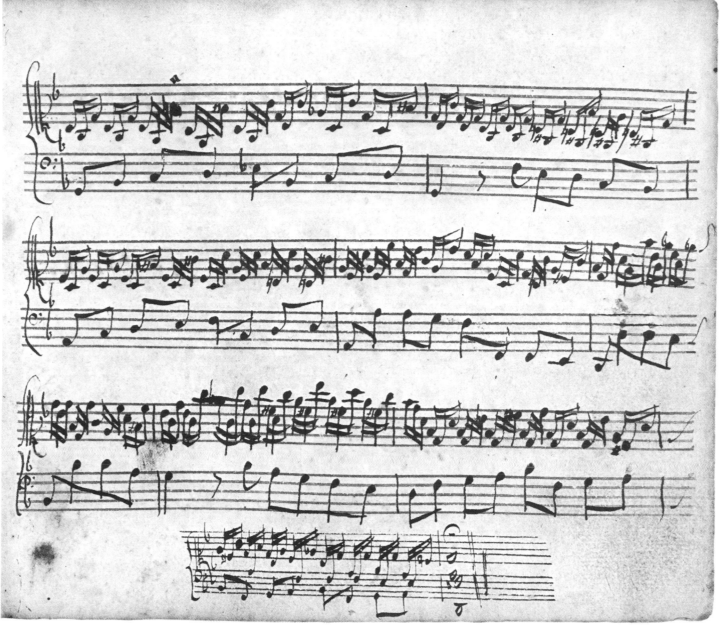

Praeludium 4.

37

volti Xa:

Praeludium. 6.

Praeludium.

Praeludium.

Praeludium

Pièce pour le Clavecin, composée par J. C. Richter.
Allemande.

56

Courante.

58

59

Praeludium. ex ♮

Praeludium. ex dh.

Praeludium, ex eh.

Fuga . à 3.

71

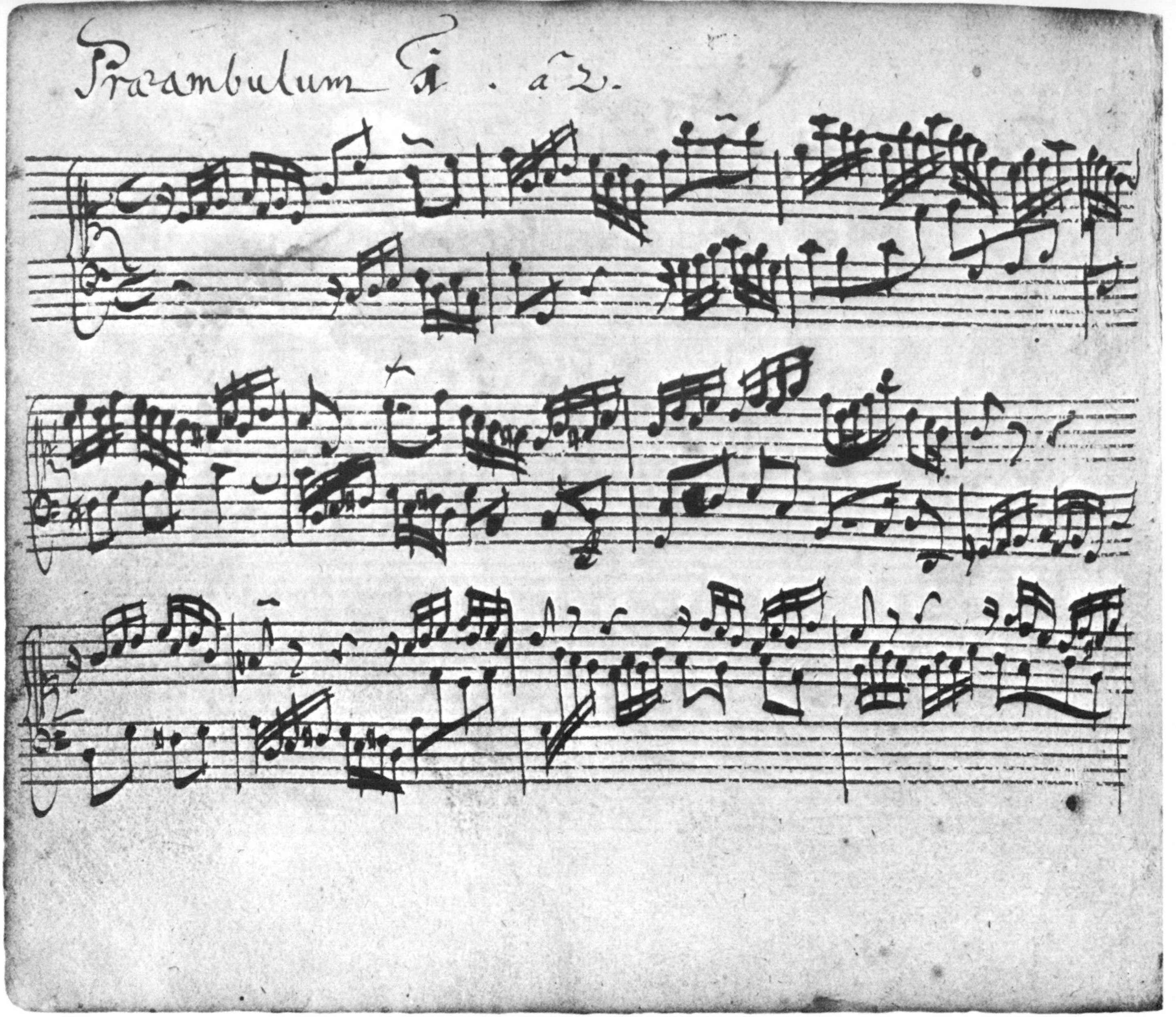
Præambulum I. à 2.

77

Præambulum. 5.

Praeambulum 6.

Praeambulum 1.

89

Præambulum 9.

Præambulum 10

93

97

Praeambulum 13.

99

Courante.

Da Capo.

Da Capo.

Gigue.

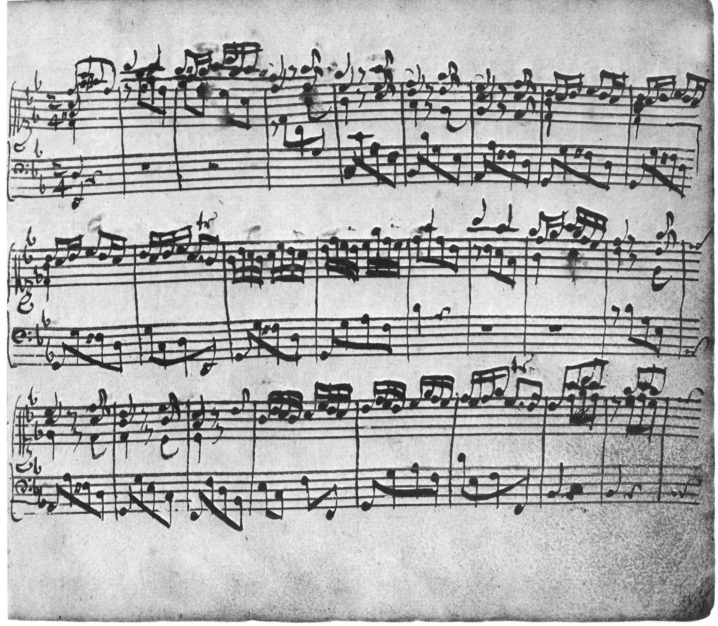

Air Italien.

Da Capo

Da Capo

Menuet Trio. di J. S. Bach.

129

Fantasia 7.

Fantasia

Fantasia 9.

Fantasia. II.

Wilhelm Friedemann

Bach

The Clavier-Büchlein measures 16½ x 19 cm. in page size, 17 x 19½ cm. in binding size, and 3 cm. in thickness. The book is bound on five vellum strips and has been reinforced at some unknown time with linen gauze. The strips are let into the boards of the front and back covers. These covers are approximately 5 mm. in thickness, and, together with the spine, are covered with one piece of thin parchment. The head and tail of the spine are worn, and the front hinge is weak; all corners are dog-eared.

The seventy-two leaves that now comprise the manuscript are bound into nine gatherings. Gathering I (pp. 3–16) embraces ff. 1–7, with ff. 6 and 7 glued in following f. 5. (The conjugate leaf to f. 1 is represented only by a stub.) The paper of f. 1 bears the watermark: HALLE.

Gathering II (pp. 17–30) embraces ff. 8–14, but a leaf has been torn out between ff. 8 and 9.

Gathering III (pp. 31–46) embraces ff. 15–22, and Gathering IV (pp. 47–62) ff. 23–30.

Gathering V (pp. 63–76) embraces ff. 31–37, but ff. 31 and 32 are glued in, and three leaves are missing between ff. 32 and 33.

Gathering VI (pp. 77–92) embraces ff. 38–45, Gathering VII (pp. 93–108) ff. 46–53, and Gathering VIII (pp. 109–124) ff. 54–61.

Gathering IX (pp. 125–146) embraces ff. 62–72, of which ff. 70 and 71 are glued in, and f. 72 sewn in as a single leaf. This last leaf has a watermark showing a crest (see p. 150).

In the present publication the Clavier-Büchlein is reproduced entire, including blank pages and photographs of both covers. (The foregoing description is based on a collation of the manuscript made by Brooks Shepard, Jr., in collaboration with Robert Metzdorf of the Yale University Library.)

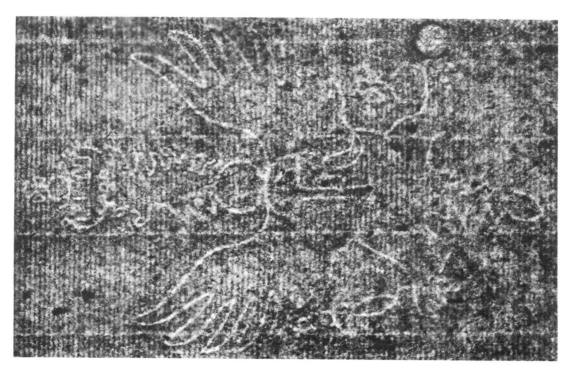

Watermark from the final end leaf.

BIBLIOGRAPHICAL NOTE

The Clavier-Büchlein has been slow to find its way into print. Not only did its long private owner-ship render it more difficult of access than those manuscripts that had passed into public institu-tions, but its principal contents were published from later and more complete sources. Not long after its purchase by the Krug family in 1845, however, C. F. Becker gave a brief account of it in Volume III of the Bachgesellschaft edition and quoted its table of ornaments. But he did not use it in establishing the text of the Inventions and Sinfonias in that volume, nor did Wilhelm Rust in his supplement. Franz Kroll also did not consult it for his text revision of the Well-Tempered Clavier in Volume XIV. Philipp Spitta saw the Clavier-Büchlein at least briefly and dealt with it in the first volume of his Bach biography published in 1873. Hans Bischoff had access to it in 1880 only just in time to take account of it in the annotations to his edition of the Inventions and Sinfonias, but in editing further works contained in the Clavier-Büchlein he was obliged to use other sources. Ernst Naumann was able to use it in transcribing for Volume XXXVI of the Bachgesellschaft edition those pieces from the Clavier-Büchlein that had not already been published from other sources; and when Alfred Dörffel prepared his supplementary text revision and publication of the remaining fragments in Volume XLV¹ the owners sent the Clavier-Büchlein to Leipzig for his use. Fragmentary though it is, Dörffel's is the best study of the Clavier-Büchlein to date.

A kind of popular edition of the completed contents, supplemented with performing indica-tions, was issued in 1927 by Hermann Keller. Since then the table of ornaments has often been published, and Ludwig Landshoff's edition of the Inventions and Sinfonias makes serious use of the Clavier-Büchlein. This facsimile edition presents the Clavier-Büchlein for the first time in its complete and original form; but the first really thorough transcription, text revision, and critical study of the Clavier-Büchlein will be the edition now in preparation for the Neue Bach Ausgabe, Serie V, Band 5, by Wolfgang Plath.

BIBLIOGRAPHY

Bach, Johann Sebastian. *Werke.* Herausgegeben von der Bach-Gesellschaft zu Leipzig. Leipzig, 1851–1899. [Reprinted, Ann Arbor, Mich., 1947.]

———*Klavierwerke.* Kritische Ausgabe mit Fingersatz und Vortragsbezeichnungen versehen von Dr. Hans Bischoff. Leipzig, [1880–1888].

———*Klavierbüchlein für Friedemann Bach.* Herausgegeben von Hermann Keller. Kassel, [1927].

———*Die 15 zweistimmigen Inventionen und die 15 dreistimmigen Sinfonien im Urtext.* Herausgegeben von Ludwig Landshoff. Leipzig, [1933].

———*Die 15 zweistimmigen Inventionen und die 15 dreistimmigen Sinfonien.* Urtext-Ausgabe. Revisionsbericht von Ludwig Landshoff. Leipzig, 1933.

———*Inventionen und Sinfonien.* Faksimile nach der im Besitz der Preussischen Staatsbibliothek in Berlin befindlichen Urschrift. [Edited by Georg Schünemann.] Leipzig, [1942].

———*Inventionen und Sinfonien.* Facsimile edition with foreword by Ralph Kirkpatrick. New York, 1948.

———*Neue Ausgabe sämtlicher Werke.* Serie V, Klavier- und Lautenwerke, Band 4, Die Klavierbüchlein für Anna Magdalena Bach (1722 und 1725). Herausgegeben von George von Dadelsen. Kassel, 1957.

———*Neue Ausgabe sämtlicher Werke.* Serie V, Band 4, Die Klavierbüchlein für Anna Magdalena

Bach. Kritischer Bericht von George von Dadelsen. Kassel, 1957.

Bach, Carl Philipp Emanuel. *Versuch über die wahre Art das Clavier zu spielen*. 2 vols. Berlin, 1753, 1762. [Facsimile reprint, edited by L. Hoffmann-Erbrecht. Leipzig, 1957.]

Danckert, Werner. "Die A-dur Suite in Friedemann Bachs Klavierbuch." *Zeitschrift für Musikwissenschaft*, VII (1924–1925), pp. 305–312.

Falck, Martin. *Wilhelm Friedemann Bach*. Leipzig, 1913.

Forkel, Johann Nikolaus. *Ueber Johann Sebastian Bachs Leben, Kunst und Kunstwerke*. Leipzig, 1802. [Facsimile reprint, with a foreword by Ralph Kirkpatrick. New York, 1950.]

Gerber, Ernst Ludwig. *Historisch-biographisches Lexicon der Tonkünstler*. Leipzig, 1790.

Grunsky, Karl. "Bachs Bearbeitungen und Umarbeiten eigener und fremder Werke." *Bach Jahrbuch*, IX (1912), pp. 61–85.

O'Meara, Eva Judd. "The Clavier-Büchlein vor Wilhelm Friedemann Bach." *Yale University Library Gazette*, VIII (1933–1934), pp. 95–99.

Schmieder, Wolfgang. *Thematisch-systematisches Verzeichniss der musikalischen Werken von Johann Sebastian Bach*. Leipzig, 1950. [Referred to as BWV.]

Spitta, Philipp. *Johann Sebastian Bach*. Leipzig, 1873, 1880.

In preparation:

Bach, Johann Sebastian. *Neue Ausgabe sämtlicher Werke*. Serie V, Klavier- und Lautenwerke, Band 5, Clavier-Büchlein vor Wilhelm Friedemann Bach. Herausgegeben von Wolfgang Plath.

———*Neue Ausgabe sämtlicher Werke*. Serie V, Band 5, Clavier-Büchlein vor Wilhelm Friedemann Bach. Kritischer Bericht von Wolfgang Plath.